Nativity & Me

SAINT SHENOUDA PRESS

Nativity Me

Fr Bishoy Kamel

ST SHENOUDA PRESS
SYDNEY, AUSTRALIA
2019

Nativity & Me

Fr Bishoy Kamel

First Edition: 2017

ST SHENOUDA PRESS
8419 Putty Rd,
Putty, NSW, 2330
Sydney, Australia

www.stshenoudapress.com

ISBN 13: 978-0-9945710-8-3

Contents

Introduction

Nativity and Me is a book written to help you explore some of the great feasts of our faith; the Feast of Annunciation, Feast of Nativity and Feast of Epiphany. These feasts are all linked by the truth of the incarnation, when Jesus took on a human body to bring salvation to all people.

More than that, this book will be an opportunity to see how these feasts are not just religious events or stories from the past, but are a living reality for Christians today. Likewise, as we consider the almost incomprehensible beauty of the incarnation, we will learn together that the incarnation also speaks to our daily lives.

Before addressing each of the feasts let's begin our exploration by considering the wonders and mysteries of the incarnation. It is our hope that Nativity and me will enrich your faith and fill your experience of these feasts with truth, meaning, joy and life!

The Incarnation of the Logos

Arguments for and against the incarnation of the Logos, our Lord Jesus Christ, have been present since the days of Saint Athanasius (c. 296– May 2, 373). Until today many people have different beliefs about the incarnation, which is why this topic should be examined and understood precisely by all Christians in accordance with the Orthodox faith.

Our understanding of the incarnation of the Logos begins with the words of Saint John in the first chapter of his Gospel where he speaks of the Incarnation of the Logos being the Word being God;

"In the beginning was the Word, and the Word was with God, and the Word was God.... The Word became flesh and made his dwelling among us. We have seen his glory, the glory of the one and only Son, who came from the Father, full of grace and truth." (John 1:1,14)

Any discussion of the incarnation of the Logos will usually include a phrase such as: 'Our Lord Jesus Christ came down from heaven to earth'. This concept is recited many times in church, particularly in the Divine Liturgy. From a human perspective, this implies that Jesus came down from heaven and left heaven vacant. We might ask how can this be? Don't we believe that God sits on His throne in heaven forever and ever, yet at the same time He has come down to Earth? This is one of the most common sources of confusion for believers to this day.

Mostly our attempts to understand this apparent contradiction are based on a human perspective; disregarding God's word, power and might to do the impossible. We should not compare or limit God from a human perspective, since we are His creation. For example, if I was to say 'I'm upstairs in my home and then I went downstairs', we would rightly assume that I was no longer upstairs since I obviously went downstairs! Clearly we cannot be upstairs and downstairs at the same time—we are human and cannot be in two places at once. This is a limitation of humanity but it does not apply to God. Only when we apply human logic to a limitless God then we get confused.

God is everywhere and sees everything, but one could ask how? God has said simply about himself, that He is the great 'I AM'. We being human cannot be everywhere and see everything—there is a distinction between humanity and God, or between the creation and the Creator.

In addition, God's home (heaven) is not like our temporary homes on earth. God's heavenly kingdom lives forever and ever. Thus, I hope we have established that God can be everywhere and see everything from the beginning to the end of time. He had no trouble being incarnated on earth and sitting on the throne in heaven!

God existing in the womb and also everywhere

Let's continue addressing areas of confusion around the incarnation and look specifically at the role of Saint Mary the Theotokos. God chose to be incarnate of the Holy Spirit by becoming a baby in the womb of Saint Mary. To say this was a big responsibility for Saint Mary is an understatement. One can only imagine what she was feeling and thinking while carrying our Lord Jesus Christ in her womb. While we may never truly comprehend what it was like to bear this great responsibility, we can be eternally grateful to Saint Mary for bringing salvation to earth.

The question or confusion regarding God existing in the womb and yet also being present everywhere at the same time, is similar to the confusion of how God could be incarnate on earth and yet exist in heaven? In addition, we have the issue of whether Jesus was simply just a human, or as our Christian dogma declares that He was God Incarnate in physical human body.

It's important to know what Christian doctrine believe, especially when heretics like Nestorius have wrongly preached that Saint Mary gave birth to Jesus as a mere human. Nestorius wanted to remove the belief that "Christ's divinity never departed from His humanity" (one might recognise this statement professed by the priest in the final confession before Holy Communion in the Coptic liturgy). Nestorius also refused to use the title 'Saint Mary the Theotokos' (Mother of God), due to his incorrect belief and understanding. Thus, we too need to be wary in order to correctly understand that Jesus was God in human body and attained His humanity alongside His everlasting divinity—He was unique among all humans. Even when He was newly born from Saint Mary's womb, His title was the King of the Jews. In the midnight praises in the Coptic church we profess that although God came down from heaven being incarnate in human body, He still retained His glorious divinity and heavenly kingship. He tasted every human hunger, thirst and pain—He resembled mankind in everything except committing sin. This difference shows us again that His divinity was intact with His humanity.

Christ cruelly crucified

To be crucified in the first century was the worst punishment and shame that could be inflicted on a person who broke the law. One may find it difficult to understand why Jesus would choose to be crucified. Saint Athanasius explains Christ's crucifixion this way:

"Firstly, God did not send Himself to the cross. Instead the Jews and Scribes sought this punishment and gained Pontius Pilate's reluctant approval to sentence Christ to crucifixion. I want to emphasise 'reluctant' as Pontius Pilate gave the Jews and Scribes the option to free our Lord Jesus Christ instead of Barabbas, and in the end the people cried 'crucify Him', we want Barabbas to be free."

Saint Athanasius explains further that Jesus allowed crucifixion to be His 'punishment' rather than anything else, for two reasons:

1. The strength of Jesus allowed Him to overcome the difficult challenge and punishment that He faced — especially since He knew His glorious resurrection to come. What concerned Him was the salvation of His children and the world, thus He remained silent when being falsely accused and requested to suffer the pains of crucifixion.

2. Jesus had to shed His blood for the remission of our

sins. That is why He could not simply die peacefully in a home or with His disciples. He had to die publicly on the cross so that His resurrection to follow would be professed publicly, removing the doubts of His disciples.

Saint Athanasius challenges people who doubt Jesus' divinity and humanity, pointing out that many Jews professed their faith in the death and Resurrection of Jesus Christ. Subsequently Christian believers should not doubt and refuse this belief.   Saint Athanasius also highlights that the Holy Bible clearly supports no separation between Christ's divinity and humanity.

He reminds us that when a person has a living soul, they have an independence to do what they want. However when a human dies, they no longer have this independence. Contrastingly when our Lord Jesus Christ arose from the dead, He had the independence to command His disciples and apostles to do certain things. For example, He commanded His disciples to preach to the whole world. Therefore if the disciples and apostles did not see the resurrected Christ, arguably they would not have followed Him. The obedience of the disciples and apostles to Jesus proves to us that our Lord Jesus Christ is eternal and alive after His death on the cross.

On believing

Let's consider the strength of our faith as Christians, and

be inspired by the lives of devout Christians including monks or nuns who leave everything behind to serve and live for the Lord. They strongly believe that God is truly eternal and leave the world to live with Him forever.

Now let's consider our Lord's resurrection. No one actually witnessed the moment our Lord was resurrected, instead only seeing that the stone where Christ was lain had been rolled away and that the tomb was empty. Yet as Christians we do not doubt that our Lord Jesus Christ did rise on the third day, as He said, and then later appeared to Mary Magdalene and His disciples. The Bible makes this clear—people saw our Jesus after He was resurrected and believed, without necessarily witnessing the exact moment of His resurrection.

In the divine liturgy in the Coptic church we may not notice that we recite a particular sentence because it's repeated so frequently. This statement, "You seated, stand up" was initially inspired from Judaism and then included in our Orthodox church. While it may not be apparent whether it matters if a person is sitting or standing in the church, this statement reminds us of a very powerful truth that in church we are before our Lord Jesus Christ and give Him upmost respect. This simple statement is another example of faith in action and the attempt of the Orthodox Church to lead us to worship the Lord without ceasing. We are reminded that Jesus is always with us. Since the moment of our baptism we are united with the Lord and He is always with us. Also, from the invocation of the Holy Spirit to transform the bread and wine we are present to the true body and blood of our Lord Jesus Christ, the eternal King of Kings.

Humanity and divinity

If we believe in God's humanity, we must believe in God's divinity and vice versa. Additionally, if we believe in God's humanity and divinity it follows that we will also believe in His love for us and all humanity, and subsequently that we will love humanity as well. God gave His only begotten Son for you and me—what amazing love this is!

In the incarnation, God took the responsibility to become man as a means to becoming the perfect human sacrifice for the salvation of mankind. When we really believe in God's humanity and divinity, we believe that He loves all people, and that we should love all people also. His loving sacrifice gives us value and responsibility in our Christian lives. We become people of purpose, motivated to sensitively care and sacrifice to others.

The spiritual person is an empathetic person

Let's explore this idea of our purpose and responsibility flowing from the divinity and humanity of Christ seen in the incarnation. The more we integrate this belief and follow the example of Jesus, the more we will find ourselves loving others and feeling their pain. A close and personal relationship with God will be seen by being empathetic to other people's feelings and a willingness to care for them. This Christ-like sensitivity has to grow outwards from our faith through the spheres of our families, churches, communities and then to the entire world.

Our appreciation of the needs of others is strengthened when we remember that we serve God Incarnate. He became as a man for the sake of mankind and experienced all the same human attributes, such as hunger and thirst, joy and sadness. Egyptian readers will have the added understanding that our Lord Jesus Christ drank from the water of the Great Nile and that He walked on Egyptian soil. The current tourist sites of where Jesus and His family lived in Egypt affirm this belief and constantly bear witness. This is really an ongoing reminder of the incarnation, in which He who was beyond time and space chose to enter creation to share our human experiences and environment.

In taking time to emphasis these aspects of the incarnation, we are reaffirming the strength and vitality of Orthodox dogma, that it is steadfast and not easily discarded or destroyed like some tangible plastic bag! Let's continue to advocate for these essential truths.

The blessing of serving

Another aspect of incarnation is the practical service

Jesus gave to others as an example to us all. In the story of the Lord blessing the five loaves and two fish, the people could have been asked to fend for themselves, perhaps gaining sustenance from the wheat that grew in the area. Instead, our Lord performed the miracle of multiplying food out of His love for His Father in Heaven and mankind. Can you imagine a priest doing the divine liturgy without bread and wine? Of course not. Similarly, to this miracle, one could ask where did the priest get the bread and wine? From the deacons that serve humbly in the church. Flowing from their practical service through the Holy Spirit, the bread and wine become the true body and blood of our Lord Jesus Christ.

To summarise, the Greek word 'zoulia' means work that helps me keep account, while the word 'erhasia' means work that does not validate me. In other words, we do not work for the sake of working or to elevate ourselves, but to glorify our Father in Heaven. Remember that Jesus taught us that we cannot serve two masters. When we work, we must not forget that Jesus is with us in all we do. Therefore we must choose whether we work to glorify Him or not.

Saint Athanasius, one of the fathers most associated with this topic, provides inspiration about how the incarnation can influence our daily lives. According to Saint Athanasius, if we believe that God was incarnate we believe that God is:

- the lover of mankind

- sensitive to all

- willing to take responsibility for the salvation of all

He glorified His Father in Heaven when He came to earth for the salvation of everyone through his crucifixion and resurrection. Saint Athanasius noted that Jesus positioned His arms open wide on the cross to represent His acceptance of responsibility for saving both Jews and Gentiles. In His crucified and resurrected body, He accomplishes the salvation of all humanity offering us all the opportunity to be reunited with God and the promise of eternity in Heaven with Him.

The Journey of the Divine Incarnation

Let us continue to explore in greater depth the journey of the incarnation of Jesus Christ, how it transcends all we know and experience, and how it speaks to our lives today.

In the incarnation:

- He who is limitless, took on the limitations of a human body.
- The everlasting was born at a specific time and place.
- He who is eternal became subject to the authority of time.
- Christ entered into time to give us the grace to enter eternity

- He took on our nature so that we can take on His.

In the limited space of her womb, the Virgin carried the Unlimited—the eternal fixed a birthday for Himself. Within Saint Mary the woman, eternal life was conceived to be given to the entire human race. This is the mystery of mysteries, the mystery of incarnation.

The Coptic Church believes in the unity of nature. Through faith we know, "It is no longer I who live, but Christ who lives in me", and that we are members of the Body of Christ, and unity with Christ leads us to say, "I have been crucified with Christ". Likewise also we are resurrected through Christ, and can say He has, "raised me up and made me sit in heavenly places" and "I do the works of Christ."

Also, through the unity of His nature Christ has united human activity - the works which Christ did while in the body—whether prayer, mercy, love, suffering and time with His eternal divinity. (i.e. the deeds of Christ while within time are united with eternity). Thus a key aspect of Incarnation is that time was united with eternity in the person of Christ. All of us who believe—frail, limited humans—became a dwelling for the unlimited Christ. Though under the authority of time, we will live forever through Christ.

The Holy Liturgy

It is the presence of Christ—in the Body—fixed in time, which is also rescuing us from the authority of time, to where we live with the angels around the throne of God in eternity. Prayer or the Holy Liturgy is the window through which we catch a glimpse of this eternity.

Prayer is converting 'dead' time into an eternal divine deed; the motion of the clock is swapped for the movement of the Spirit. The Spirit at prayer calls us to participate with the spirits of the saints in eternity, because by coming closer to Christ, we come closer to the kingdom of heaven.

The hermits are humans like us, but through their many prayers and by clinging to the Lord, they exited the boundaries of time and space, as the Apostle Paul says: "I know such a man—whether in the body or out of the body I do not know, God knows— how he was caught up into Paradise and heard inexpressible words, which it is not lawful for a man to utter." (2 Corinthians 12:2)

The utensils and materials used for the Mysteries of the Church, are filled with divine characteristics when sanctified by prayers. Daily human functions (like eating and drinking) gain unlimited blessings. Our worldly deeds, no matter how offensive, gain blessings through prayers—they are cleansed from worry, selfishness and bad qualities such as lying and deceit. They become sanctified and appropriate to be offered to God, with all other religious services.

The incarnation took us out of our time-limited capabilities to divine, unlimited, out of time capabilities, so I can say with the Apostle: "I can do everything in Christ who strengthens me", and through faith in Christ, who was united with my human nature, I can move mountains.

The Incarnation took me out of the boundaries of materialistic richness—which depends on the limits of personality, money, health and time—to the unlimited richness, "that though He was rich, yet for your sakes He became poor, that you through His poverty [His Incarnation] might become rich." (2 Corinthians 8:9). Also, "My grace is sufficient for you, for My strength is made perfect in weakness, for when I am weak, then I am strong." (2 Corinthians 12:9)

The Continuing Incarnation

Having established the power and vitality of the Incarnation to transcend time and space, let's look at some of the evidence that shows the continuation of Incarnation in our experience.

First proof — the same body

The Lord Jesus, who took on our human body through

the Virgin Mary, is still with that Body in heaven and till the end of the age. He will come on the clouds with the same body which He took from us, and every eye will see that body—the marks of the nails and the spear in His side! Incarnation is the unity of God—without mingling or mixing—with our humanity, till the end of time.

Second proof — at the altar

This is very important—the true Body and Blood of Christ is always present on the altar, with the priest confessing with a loud voice, even to the last breath: "This is the body which He took from our Lady, the Lady of us all, the holy Theotokos, Saint Mary." It is the Body that: "He gave up for us upon the wood of the cross, of His own free will for us all." When we partake of the body and blood of Christ we continuously live his incarnation.

Third proof—the church is the body of Christ

The Incarnation is continued through the Church which is the body of Christ, and we are all members in the body as we read in the Scriptures: "And He put all things under His feet, and gave Him to be head over all things to the church, which is His body, the fullness of Him who fills all in all." (Ephesians 1: 22, 23).

Living the Incarnation

Having seen how the Incarnation remains real for us today, let's look at keys for continuously living in the Incarnation,

Baptism and Incarnation

We know the timeline of the Virgin's Annunciation and the divine pregnancy, which we could align for ourselves going through Baptism: "...that you put off, concerning your former conduct, the old man which grows corrupt according to the deceitful lusts, and be renewed in the spirit of your mind, and that you put on the new man which was created according to God, in true righteousness and holiness." {Ephesians. 4: 22, 23).

Discovering the truth about this birth means understanding life through the lens of divine Incarnation or the new birth in Christ. Many of us think about baptism as just a memory, but actually it is the beginning of our birth in the Spirit. Baptism is the divine Annunciation when we became heavenly citizens, it is the start of my membership in the Body of Christ, and continues forever! The death of the flesh is not a stumbling block, because it is a birth from above – it is a continuation of the incarnation. Do we live our baptism every day? As the Scriptures say, "Or do you not know that as many of us as were baptised into Christ Jesus were baptised into His death? Therefore we were buried with Him through baptism into death, that just as Christ was raised from the dead by the glory of the Father, even so we also should walk in newness of life." (Romans 6: 3,4)

If we are dead through the old man, but alive in Christ, can we change our natural birth from our father and mother? What about our new birth through the Holy Trinity? Baptism never changes or ends and so while death ends my physical relationship with my parents, my relationship with the Body of Christ does not end, once I have died with Him. I am now alive forever, through Him, because He is alive forever.

Let us taste daily the new life through baptism as a source which overflows always, without end, leading to eternal life, and this is achieved through continuous repentance every day, to renew the mind and wash the soul—the perpetual work of baptism.

Incarnation took place when the Holy Spirit descended upon the Virgin, purifying her. Then she fell pregnant with the Son of God Incarnate, the Divine Body. During the Liturgy, the Holy Spirit descends upon the priest and the congregation—purifying them, then upon the bread and wine turning it into the body and blood of the Lord. The action of Incarnation is accomplished in a united nature, in order that we can eat and live.

In all of this we can see how the repentant soul lives out daily the divine Incarnation, being sanctified by the Holy Spirit and abiding in the Body of Christ as they come to the altar. The priest calls out loudly (in the words of Jesus Christ), come and eat, "This is my body". This is the same body our Lady, Saint Mary, gave birth to, which was made one with His divinity. Now we have the unlimited presence of Jesus which He grants to the repentant, to live out the mystery of Incarnation at all times and also to eat of his slain body.

I cannot live without Him

Just as the parts of our body—the hand, leg or eye—are alive likewise I have to live daily in the divine Incarnation: "It is no longer I who live, but Christ who lives in me" (Galatians 2: 20). Also, as we read earlier from Ephesians, "And He put all things under His feet, and gave Him to be head over all things to the church, which is His body, the fullness of Him who fills all in all." (Ephesians 1:22-23)

To further emphasise our unity with the Incarnate Body of Christ, the Apostle Paul also instructs: "Shall I then take the members of Christ and make them members of a harlot? Certainly not!" (1 Corinthians 6:15). Thus to live the Incarnation continuously we have to remember nothing separates us from Christ, that we are to say "let it be according to Your will, not mine" and to have no other mind except that of Christ—"But we have the mind of Christ" (1 Corinthians 2:16), and for us "to live is Christ" (Philippians 1:21).

Membership of the unseen body of Christ

The fullness of Him who fills everything, helps me to 'feel' the feelings of all the members of the Body, so that living the Incarnation means feeling the joy and pain of other members—"Rejoice with those who rejoice, and weep with those who weep" (Romans 12:15). We should also work with others for the unity of the body: "And He Himself gave some to be apostles, some prophets, some evangelists, and some pastors and teachers, for the equipping of the saints for the work of ministry, for the edifying of the body of Christ." (Ephesians 4:11, 12)

The Incarnation is a continuous building of the body which is the Church and a continuous abiding of the members together with the head. The practical test of the Incarnation is to live our day to day lives abiding with our brothers and sisters in the Body of Christ, sharing in their joy, worries and sufferings. As the Apostle Paul said, "...and fill up in my flesh what is lacking in the afflictions of Christ, for the sake of His body, which is the church" (Colossians 1:24). There will be constant activity in our lives to edify the Body of Christ, living our lives as branches in the vine, giving and taking, and as a member in the body—working, helping, cooperating and living in unity.

The hidden life of Christ in humans

Through the Incarnation the life of Jesus is present and growing in the Christian's life. We are united with His body and so we are:

- born with Him
- tested by Satan—but victorious

- immersed in the Jordan River in baptism
- hung on the Cross
- resurrected with Him
- ascended with Him
- seated in heavenly places with Him.

Looking at it from another way, Jesus Christ has passed through this world in our body. He faced the devil and his trials, and overcame, the sins of the world through His death on the cross and finally being raised from the dead. In this way the Incarnation is the beginning of the ladder of a glorified life. Those who continually struggle dying to the world, rising up from sin and lifting the mind towards heaven are the ones who are continuously living the divine Incarnation.

It is written in the book of Philokalia concerning this subject:

"The life of our Lord Jesus Christ is actually the Christian life which starts with every Christian. Then it grows leading him to perfection, through the good will of God the Father, and the work of the Spirit dwelling in the Christian person, under the guidance of Lord Jesus Himself, who promised to live inside us during all the ages. This life is not only possible for all Christians, but it is a must. The chosen among them are the ones who go deep in the depth of the secret life of Christ, then gradually climb up its steps."

Following Christ's steps

Jesus lived in the same way as all children do and He blessed childhood living in its most beautiful form. He grew to live as a youth and so blessed this stage of life too, showing it in the purest and strongest form.

The earthly Father of Jesus, Joseph the Carpenter, is thought to have died when Jesus was still young, around the age of 15, certainly before his public ministry began. Jesus then worked as a carpenter Himself and provided for His mother. By doing this He blessed work and dealt with both all types of people—which raises an interesting thought—how did He deal with all kinds of people? How did He deal with blasphemers? How did He relate to His Mother? How did He manage His worldly duties such as paying the required temple tax of all adult Jews? How did He tolerate the injustice of the wicked and the accusation of being a 'Nazarene? How did He deal with these and other human interactions?

It may help us to consider that if Jesus Christ was living among us today, in His Incarnated Body, He would have attended school, got a job and worked.... We can try and imagine in our own time period, how He would relate to family, friends and colleagues? What His behaviour would be like and, even what would He wear?

This is the life of God who was incarnated for our sake, who gave us an example to follow—to live our lives following the footsteps of the Lord from childhood till old age, , saying: "For me, to live is Christ" because He resembled us in everything except sin.

This is the way to experience the Incarnation all the days of our life, and to experience the power of Christ and the leadership of the Holy Spirit.

Continuous presence with God

Practising the continuous presence of God also points us to the Incarnation. The continuous feeling of the presence with God with us in all our deeds and activities signals the divine Incarnation because we sense Him in all we do day by day; "for in Him we live and move and have our being." (Acts 17: 28)

The destitute and needy

It is a wonderful part of the Incarnation that we discover Jesus whenever we care for those who are poor or in need: "I was hungry and you gave me food... I was naked and you clothed me." (Matthew 25: 35)

The Church and its prayer

The schedule of prayer as directed by the Church further supports us to continuously live the Incarnation.

During the month of Kiahk all the prayers, meditations and hymns relate to the Incarnation from the perspective of our Lady the Virgin.

Also, the daily prayers of the Theotokias address the way in which the Virgin was offered to God as representative of humanity in the mystery of Incarnation.

Joy in the Incarnation

The Annunciation of the Incarnation was full of joy and happiness. Happiness is like a thermometer for the Christian, and can be found in relation to the comprehension of the mystery of the Incarnation. Let us look more closely at the reality of joy as an evidence and outcome of the Incarnation.

"The life was manifested, and we have seen, and bear witness, and declare to you that eternal life which was with the Father and was manifested to us.... And these things we write to you that your joy may be full." (1 John 1:2,4)

There is a difference between worldly joy and the joy of the Incarnation. Temporary worldly joy is the result of social, economic and physical circumstances surrounding a person, and is subject to many dangers, not the least among them being death.

On the other hand, Christian joy is a result of the presence of God and His unity with our nature, even if the social, economic and physical circumstances are difficult. For example, seeing the challenging events surrounding the birth of Jesus when there was no room in the inn and He was laid in a manger. Christians, our joy in the birth of Christ is a result of the presence of God among us regardless of the circumstances. We reach the pinnacle of that joy when we comprehend the depth of the love of God on the cross. Other examples of joy include the Three Saintly Youth praising God amidst the blazing fire (Daniel 3:24-26). Paul the Apostle was singing while in prison, "Rejoice in the Lord". (Philippians 3:1). In these examples we see that joy is inseparable from Incarnation; "Your joy no one will take from you." (John 16: 22}. Not even death can separate us from Christian joy because God was Incarnated and united with our nature.

Fulness of joy—life undefeated by death

Jesus Christ gives us Himself and He is life eternal. The grave which we all will enter is simply a place for the body which returns to dust.

History is full of saints who declared that life in them was stronger than death. In fact some of them faced death joyfully as if death was something weak, while "others were tortured, not accepting deliverance" (Hebrews 11: 35) such as the 49 elders of Scetis. Others were raised up after death because He who was in them is stronger than death, such as St George who died three times! These saints mocked death (the last enemy) saying "where is your sting?"

Thus we see the Christian who has discovered that Christ gives eternal life, in full joy, which death cannot destroy. Rather death only adds to the bliss and perfection of the joy we have in Jesus.

Fulness of joy—overcoming sin

The life of Christ that is within us is stronger than sin and we can also be sure that Jesus has carried the penalty for that sin in His own body while on the cross. Even if we fall into sin today because of our weakness, "the Blood of Jesus Christ His Son cleanses us from all sin." (1 John 1: 7). Each time we offer repentance and partake of the Blood of Jesus we repeat with the Apostle, "...who loved us and washed us from our sins in His own Blood." (1 Revelation 1:5) So we can strongly rejoice because the blood of Christ has totally overcome sin.

Fulness of joy—victory over the world

"He who is in you is greater than he who is in the world." (1 John 4:4). "Be of good cheer I have overcome the world." (John 16:33). Those who live the Incarnation, a life of repentance, carrying the cross and following Jesus, will feel unlimited, divine power in overcoming the world. This experience is like when David felt the power of God in conquering Goliath. In this context, we define the 'world' in the same way as the Apostle when he says: "For all that is in the world—the lust of the flesh, the lust of the eyes, and the pride of life." (1 John 2:16)

Fulness of joy—overcoming the devil

Jesus Christ, who lives inside those who live the incarnation, overcame the devil on the Mount of Temptation. He crushed the devil through the cross and descended into Hades, releasing those who were held captive. By this we know that the devil has no authority to take any soul to Hades as he previously did. That is why the Lord says to the thief: "Today you will be with Me in Paradise." (Luke 23:43) That is why we can rejoice with the Apostle saying: "O Death, where is your sting? O Hades, where is your victory?" (1 Corinthians15:55).

Fulness of joy—for all of life

Eternal life is not limited to the death of a person, but believers are living eternal life now in the body. Knowing Jesus Christ allows, a life of unity with God, of victorious life over the world and its lust. Because He who is inside us is stronger than sin and the prince of this world as Christ crushed the devil and overcame death.

As for love, it is the very nature of God, as we read—"God is love". It is because of love that He entered the womb of St. Mary, made Himself of no reputation, taking the form of a bondservant, and became, subject to time. Eternal life is a flowing love which fills our lives, the love of being united with the beloved in fullness towards God and humanity. May we live love in all fullness so that we live in the light. "The Lord my God will enlighten my darkness." (Psalm 18:28). He is the One who disperses darkness and adds indescribable joy to our souls. He is the Incarnate light of truth and purity who disperses the darkness of evil and impurity. He is the light of love for everyone, dispersing all envy, evil and fanaticism. He is the light of the divine Incarnation: "In Him was life, and the life was the light of men. And the light shines in the darkness." (John 1:4,5)

All of what we are describing is our birthright in Christ who took our body and became human, taking what is ours and giving us what is His. Let us:

- Be filled with His life and live it

- Be filled with His love and enjoy it

- Be filled with His light that our lives may be enlightened.

Greatness of God's descent to be with humanity

As we complete our study of the journey of Incarnation, let's take a moment to reflect in a more devotional way on all that is caught up in this mysterious and wonderful Christian truth.

Christ was born on Earth, yet He was born from eternity; He was born of a woman, yet she was a virgin—thus the divinity and humanity were united in Christ who has no father on earth nor a mother in heaven. His mother carried Him in her womb, but the Prophet (John the Baptist) knew Him while still in his mother Elizabeth's womb and he trembled with joy for the arrival of Christ the Word, his Creator. He was wrapped in swaddling clothes but came out of the shrouds in His resurrection. He slept in a manger yet the angels glorified Him, a star announced His birth and the Magi worshipped Him.

Concerning the Jews He had no appearance of beauty, yet for David He was fairer than the sons of men—He glowed on the mountain brighter than the sun. He was baptised as a human and waived punishment for sin as God. He was tempted as a human and overcame as God. He calls us to have faith as He has overcome the world. He was hungry yet He fed the multitudes, He is the Living Bread of heaven. He was thirsty, yet He cried out saying: "If anyone thirsts, let him come to Me and drink" (John 7:37). He promised to those who believe in Him that rivers of living water will flow out of their hearts.

He suffered and was tired, but He is rest for the tired and heavy-burdened. He was caught in the storm yet walked on water, rebuked the wind and saved Peter who was about to drown. He paid the temple tax having got the money from a fish's belly even though He is the master of those asking Him to pay the tax. He rose early to pray, prayed through the night, sweat drops of blood while praying, and yet it is He who answers the prayers of all of us who call upon the name of the Lord.

He wept yet He is the one who dries the tears of those

who cry. He asked where Lazarus was buried, showing His humanity, but then revived him as He is God. He was sold cheaply—for just 30 silver coins—but He bought humanity with the precious price of His blood. He was led as a sheep to the slaughter and yet He is the Shepherd of Israel and of the entire world. His presence was announced by a voice crying in the wilderness and yet He is the Word through whom all things were created! He was sick and wounded yet He cures every illness and wound. He was denied justice and crucified on the wood of the cross, yet He is restoring our rights. He was given the bitter taste of vinegar to drink, yet He is the one turning water into wine. He delivered up His spirit at His death, when the veil of the sanctuary was torn apart, and rocks were broken, yet the dead arose from the tombs.

He died but now He is the one giving life—He destroyed death by His death. He was buried yet He arose. He descended into Hades yet delivered the souls of the righteous. He ascended into heaven and will come again to judge the living and the dead!

Let us continue exploring the depths of meaning and mystery in the Incarnation through the words of St John Chrysostom:

What can I say? How should I talk? Miracles like these stun me and I can say nothing. The Ancient of Days became a baby. He who is sitting on the throne in the highest heavens is lying in a manger—the impossible, the profound, the, is touched by human hands. He who releases the bondages of sin is tied up in swaddling clothes, due to His will. He has decided to turn lousiness into honour, to clothe shame with glory and to show that the borders of humility are the borders of power. Therefore I can endure physical humiliation to be united with the eternal Word. He took my flesh and gave me His Spirit, and through giving and taking He is preparing me for the treasure of life. He took my flesh to sanctify me, He gave me His Spirit to redeem me. St John Chrysostom, Homily 2 on the Nativity, No. 2.

"And the Word became flesh and dwelt among us". After Saint John has said that those who believe in His Name are born of God, he explains to us the inexpressible honour which is, "the Word became flesh" and that the Lord took the form of a bondservant. He made Himself the Son of Man while in truth He is the Son of God, to make people sons of God. When the One seated on high looks down on the lowly, this does not harm His glory in any way. His aim is to lift the lowly from his poverty—nothing of His divine nature was lost, instead He has promoted us to inexpressible glory. We, who were always in shame and darkness...

This is what happens when a king talks to a poor beggar in kindness and care. He is not diminishing his honour in any way, but rather gives the beggar honour and respect before others. St John Chrysostom, Homily 11 on the Gospel of John

As we conclude this chapter let us consider some final points about the Incarnation.

Jesus took our body by being born of a woman so that in that body he would be subject to death and that is why Christ died. However this body, because of its unity with the Word, was not subject to corruption according to nature, and that is why Christ arose, completing two wondrous acts at the same time:

1. Completing the death of us all in His own body—"If One died for all, then all died." (2 Corinthians 5:14.

2. Eliminating death and corruption through the unity of the Word of God with the body, because the Word is not subject to corruption, so too the body was incorruptible (that is why He arose from among the dead).

And so, the Word took our body, to redeem us from the sting of death, and reconciling us with the Father through His Blood. He participated with us in everything except sin, becoming our brother and calling us to be His children saying: "Our Father who art in heaven". That is why it was essential for the Son of God to be the Son of Man: "For many deceivers have gone out into the world who do not confess Jesus Christ as coming in the flesh. This is a deceiver and an antichrist." (2 John 1:7).

"The Word of God was not limited in a Body, but He rather used the Body." Athanasius the Apostolic

Feasts and the Incarnation

Having laid deep foundations for our understanding of and belief in the Incarnation, we will now focus on three key 'Incarnation' moments in the life of Jesus that we celebrate through the Feast of Annunciation, Feast of Nativity and Feast of Epiphany.

Feast of Annunciation

The Feast of Annunciation falls on 29th Baramhat (7th April), which precedes the Nativity Feast on the 29th Kiahk (7th January) by nine months. The Church also celebrates this feast every 29th of the Coptic month so that its children may regularly renew these remarkable events and live the continuous joy of the Annunciation of the Incarnation, Nativity and Resurrection. A question we can ask ourselves is "do we take the opportunity to celebrate this feast every month"? Is our life full of the joy of Annunciation?—this expression of great joy which is available to us all as announced to Mary by the angel Gabriel (Luke 1:26-38) Do we consider all things in this world as unimportant compared to the knowledge of the Annunciation of salvation? We are reminded that no person, no pain, no illness, no circumstance can take this joy from us as the Lord has said.

Not just a story to repeat

The Annunciation is not just a story which we repeat every year, nor just a sermon or a subject to study. Rather it is to be experienced and lived by every person. The apostle John speaks about the joyful Annunciation in his first epistle, saying, "That which we have seen and heard we declare to you, that you also may have fellowship with us; and truly our fellowship is with the Father and with His Son Jesus Christ. And these things we write to you that your joy may be full." (1 John 1:3) John has himself experienced this joyful Annunciation and shares with us also the Annunciation message so that our joy may be full. No one can say these words unless he is joyful and wants others around him to be joyful too.

The joy of the thief

At its heart, Christianity is a message of joy. A joyful person cannot restrict the joy which is inside their heart but is compelled to share it with others. In this way the Good News as seen in the Bible comes to the tired, destitute and pained. The prophet Isaiah and St Luke wrote, "The Spirit of the Lord is upon Me, because He has anointed Me to preach the gospel to the poor; He has sent Me to heal the broken-hearted."

The poor in this context include people like the thief at the right hand of the cross. A very strong annunciation entered his life in his last hours so that he said:

"Remember me O Lord, when You come into Your Kingdom." Could there be any joy stronger than one that even overcomes death? The thief at the right hand of Jesus felt a miraculous joy that exceeded the pain of death. He asked the Lord to remember him in words of upmost joy.

St Sidhom Bishay's joy amidst torture

Saint Sidhom Bishay was severely tortured and dragged along the ground in Damietta. While he was in extreme pain, they filled tar and mud on his face. Yet he cried out saying, "Oh kind one." In this he was calling for Saint Mary as we say in the book of the Hours (Agpia): "When my soul departs my body, attend to me." Saint Sidhom would see Saint Mary in front of him and he was so happy. Out of his great joy he forgot about all his suffering and pain.

Saint Stephen's blessing

Saint Stephen's joy was also greater than death itself: "But he, being full of the Holy Spirit, gazed into heaven and saw the glory of God, and Jesus standing at the right hand of God, and said, 'Look! I see the heavens opened and the Son of Man standing at the right hand of God!'" (Acts 7:54-56)

St Stephen started blessing those around him and saying, "Lord, do not charge them with this sin." Could anyone's face be shining as bright as an angel amidst these circumstances? How is this possible when people are stoning him and he is fighting death in the final moments of his life?

This is because the Annunciation is not just the retelling of the story where the angel comes to the Virgin and speaks to her of the Nativity. Instead, as we have seen, the Annunciation is a way of life, which the children of God have always lived and practised, regardless of circumstances.

More examples of Annunciation joy

We read in Hebrews that many saints met death joyfully, "Others were tortured, not accepting deliverance, that they might obtain a better resurrection." (Hebrews 11:35) By this we see their powerful life   which was stronger than the fear of death. Instead these and many other saints yearned for martyrdom, not wanting to escape death, seeking instead the hope set before them.

The Annunciation—this message that Jesus has come to the world to be born as a baby and live as one of us— is accompanied with an amazing offer: "Peace I leave with you, My peace I give to you; not as the world gives do I give to you." (John 14:27). God's peace is stronger than the fleeting happiness of the world which has a materialistic, impermanent nature. As we read earlier, Saint John says, "that your joy might be full". In contrast, the joy of the world is not full. Further, we know joy and peace are fruit of the Holy Spirit. Saint Paul says: "But what things were gain to me, these I have counted loss for Christ. What is more, I also count all things loss for the excellence of the knowledge of Christ Jesus my Lord, for whom I have suffered the loss of all things, and count them as rubbish, that I may gain Christ." (Philippians 3:7-8)

If you read the biographies of the church fathers and the saints, you will find them always happy amidst persecution. "So they departed from the presence of the council, rejoicing that they were counted worthy to suffer shame for His name." (Acts 5:41) When a person loses something for the Name of Christ, he is a victorious because he has gained Christ. If people reproach you saying that you are on the losing end, your answer instead should be that you have gained Christ. The Lord says: "Your joy no one will take from you."

Someone might ask: "How can we live a life of constant joy if we sometimes get angry and fall into various tribulations?" Here Jesus talks about spiritual joy, a joy in Christ which one can take from you regardless of your circumstances.

It's important to differentiate between material and spiritual joy. Christians can experience material loss, illness or hardship but remain joyful because their joy is a spiritual rather than materialistic. This joy is a fruit of the Holy Spirit. Finally, in the Beatitudes, Jesus does not tell us to tolerate various challenges; instead He says, "Rejoice and be exceedingly glad" (Matthew 5:12).

The sinful woman leaves in joy

What is the truth at the centre of the story of the sinful woman? She was a woman who spent her life doing evil, until she met Christ. We don't know exactly how she met Him but our Lord Jesus said, "Her sins, which are many, are forgiven; for she loved much: but to whom little is forgiven, the same loves little." (Luke 7:47) Sin is one of the causes of depression for a human being. The annunciation for the forgiveness of sins is a message of true joy. Similar to the thief on the cross, the sinful woman was washed in the Blood of Christ. How joyful are people when they realise their sins are forgiven?! (1 John 2:12) The Apostle says in his Epistle, "I write to you because your sins are forgiven." In the same epistle of Saint John, it also says, "If we say that we have no sin, we deceive ourselves, and the truth is not in us. If we confess our sins, He is faithful and just to forgive us our sin." (1 John 1:8, 9) Also, "The blood of Jesus Christ His Son cleanses us from all sin." (1 John 1:7)

This sinful woman had no hope whatsoever when coming before our Lord. Yet in meeting Christ, the Lord said to her, "Your sins are forgiven, go in peace." This is the true message of salvation; the message of joy. This woman came out of the house of Simon the Pharisee with great joy and happiness.

Her joy was an inner joy, as the Bible says about her, "and she began to wash His feet with tears and wiped them with the hairs of her head, and she kissed His feet, and anointed them with fragrant oil." During the annunciation the Church chose to mention the sinful woman who went back home joyfully because her sins were forgiven. She was so joyful that she could not stop her tears from pouring.

On the 29th Baramhat, we commemorate both the Annunciation and the Resurrection of Christ. In this way we see that the power of the Annunciation is underscored by the Resurrection.

The Feast of Nativity

Christmas for many people is the highlight of the year, which is fitting because the Nativity of the Lord Jesus Christ is a feast for all of humanity, just as the angel told the shepherds, "I bring you good tidings of great joy which will be to all people. For there is born to you this day in the City of David a Saviour, who is Christ the Lord." (Luke 2:10,11) This feast is for everybody in the entire world. At Christmas we are not celebrating the birthday of a great personality, prophet or father of fathers, but we are celebrating a divine, wondrous event which God has performed for humanity. There is a big difference between celebrating a person's birthday, no matter how high his rank is, and celebrating the Nativity.

Discovering the divine wonder

Our focus at Christmas can be to discover the divine

wonder of this event, in which God has reached out with love to humanity. Christmas is much more than celebrating someone's birthday. Instead we come into the presence of Jesus who is beyond the prophets and the angels, and can change the very nature of a person from corruption.

When we come to the Feast of Nativity we meditate on this divine, wondrous deed in which God the Logos, took on a body like us, was united with our nature, and offered us a new nature in Himself, a divine incorruptible nature..

We are all born from earthly parents and inherit a physical body of with all its weaknesses and desires. When Christ took the body of a human being through birth, He granted us a new birth with a new nature. Our human nature is subject to corruption and death, but His divine nature imparted to us by faith is eternal.

In all of this, our God seeks to lift up all of humanity and seat us with Christ on the right hand of the Father in heaven. As we remember and acknowledge this great Christmas truth, we truly become aware of the divine wonder of the birth of Christ.

The gift of the Holy Spirit

Christmas is a time for giving gifts and may also remind us of an important gift Jesus has given. On the way to His Ascension, Jesus commanded His disciples to wait and receive a heavenly gift. The gift of the Holy Spirit was to fill the body of human beings, so that we become a temple for the Spirit of God. We are then told, "Go therefore, and make disciples of all the nations, baptising them in the name of the Father and of the Son and of the Holy Spirit." (Matthew 28:19) In this, the gift we are given, we are also to give to fulfil the divine aim of the Incarnation of God.

Baptism and Nativity

The birth of Christ gave humanity a new birth which reaches us through baptism. If we are born of the water and the Spirit, we will see the kingdom of God and will have a place in heaven. In this way Christians are born twice; once to die and once to live forever. That is why Saint Paul calls Jesus 'the second Adam.'

When we receive the grace of the second birth of baptism, we receive the heavenly nature. Thus when we celebrate Nativity, we are not just remembering an ancient historical event, but are celebrating the birth of Jesus Christ inside us. All those who belong to Jesus should look at themselves in a new way, according to what the Scriptures say about our new birth. Then we will see that our nature, thoughts and emotions are heavenly, not earthly.

Lord of Glory, born in a manger

In the Nativity we see a unique mix of poverty and

wealth, earthly squalor and heavenly glory. Jesus was born in a vulnerable human body just like ours, surrounded by poverty. Through this He includes us in His divine richness. As a baby in the manger, Jesus was the embodiment of human frailty that was united with divine nature. Around the manger, we see poor shepherds alongside archangels who were singing heavenly praise. This is the wonderful discovery we have as Christians during the Feast of Nativity. At the birth of Jesus earth and heaven unite; the most abject human poverty is infused with the splendour of Divine Majesty.

Heaven shared its glory with the earth, and the archangels were praising saying, "Glory be to God in heaven, peace on earth and good will towards men." (Luke 2:14) A threefold sharing in praise occurred at that moment; heaven, earth and mankind. On that day the star guided the Magi, the angels were singing, all creation was praising,—... a wondrous divine work!

How do we respond to the Nativity?

As we have said in the Nativity, Jesus unites the heavenly with the earthly. The divine nature is united with human nature. We experience this unity when we come to Church and partake of the Body and Blood of Christ! This is a continuing impartation of God's gift to us, through the Incarnation.

Which is why, as we celebrate Nativity, it is an opportunity to reflect not only on the divine birth of Christ but on our own. We remember, "Today I have been newly born!" We might ask ourselves, has Christ been born in the manger of my life or not yet? Have I discovered that I am a new person? Have I been transformed through Jesus to a place of unlimited desire for the love of God so that we live for God until our last breath? Let us be frank with ourselves: Have we broken the wall of selfishness inside us? Has the spring of divine love flowed from our hearts?

Saint Paul says, "Therefore, if anyone is in Christ, he is a new creation; old things have passed away; behold, all things have become new." (2 Corinthians 5:17). This inspires us to take off this narrow body, heart and mind so as to feel the new birth we have in Jesus Christ today—in all our life. Why not write the verse above, always keep it with you, and let it be your meditation verse for the Nativity Feast.

This is telling us, enough is enough—the old nature has passed away. Enough living in the past and its weaknesses. This is not what Christ intends for us. We can move beyond coming to confession and saying "I am weak". We all know that in ourselves, we are weak. It is more important to be able to say, 'I am weak but Christ has worked within me and even if I am facing death I do not fear it. I am now a new creation in Christ Jesus.'

Nativity and new creation

New creation may sound too difficult—aren't we aware of the old life being active among us Christians? Don't we hold grudges, have hard hearts, and demonstrate weak love by acting selfishly?

Despite the old nature being contrary to the joy of Christmas and reality of Incarnation, we are reminded in Revelations, "I am making everything new... a new heaven and a new earth...." (Revelation 21:1, 5). Everything will be new—not only new clothes on the outside, but everything becomes new through our second birth in Christ Jesus.

If we are to live out this new creation Jesus has attained for us, we need to follow His pathway starting with the Nativity. Christ's path is very clear—it started at the manger and ended at Golgotha. As a new creation in Christ Jesus, we also go through these stages. We begin with the manger of humility and move through to carrying the cross, and ultimately Golgotha: "If anyone wants to become my disciple, he must deny himself, take up his cross and follow Me." (Matthew 16:24) In doing this, we release the power of resurrection within us, to release the life of being a new creation in Christ.

The path which began in the manger doesn't end at resurrection but continues to ascension. Our thoughts, our soul, our life ascends with Christ, as St Paul says,

"And God raised us up with Christ and seated us with him in the heavenly realms in Christ Jesus." (Ephesians 2:6) The Lord Jesus, is now sitting at the right hand of glory, with a body of flesh which is the same as ours. Our place is now in heaven as we are members of His body so. This is not a simile or metaphor, but it is the living truth.

We are to start and continue our lives in Christ via the manger of humility. This is the same humility with which Christ clothed himself when He saw evil on the earth and descended to save humanity. This is not just for when we gather at church, we should check our attitudes and behaviour at home with our family and friends. Do we relate to them from the manger of humility, or are we full of pride and arrogance? Also at work we need to be accountable for our honesty and excellence. In priesthood or Christian service, we need to review if we are on the path of humility or seeking after high positions.

A concern is that we will make a wrong start and stumble along the way that pride will cause us to lose sight of the milestones that mark the path Jesus takes. Often we hear the gospel and the voice of the church but what is our response to the word and presence of God?

We can go further—God gives us good gifts and talents yet instead we destroy them in pride. God freely offers us goodness and blessings, but instead we boast and walk the path of evil. God gives us the grace of knowledge, wisdom and a good testimony yet we respond by feeling proud and better than others.

This is why as we celebrate Nativity, Jesus the Lord of Glory calls us once again to the manger, asking us to examine ourselves and be honest. , Let us observe these spiritual feasts and meditate on the events of each occasion.

Let us be humble and vigilant the shepherds were. Let us open our hearts and look at the Nativity which has what brought love, sacrifice, courage and true humility into our world.

Who are the saints?

Saints are human beings who discovered the treasure of the Holy Spirit inside them and through it, performed many superior deeds. "If you have faith as small as a mustard seed, you will say to this mountain "move from here to there and it will move." That is why, my beloved, when we read the biographies of the saints, we read about wondrous deeds and astounding miracles. The Lord of Glory said "the works that I do you will do also, and greater works than these you will do." Meditate in the splendour that entered into our nature. We do not fear anything anymore, any person or tribulation.

We have to ornament ourselves with full Divine Humility, flee from evil in humbleness and quietness, and never be proud or haughty of our capabilities. There is a strange power filling our heart. We fear nothing, not even death. The saints used to meet death with a big smile.

A New Nature

What is this new nature?

A new nature is one which conquers death and fear. We do not even fear the future because our future is in Jesus Christ, an unlimited eternity. "For to me, to live is Christ and to die is gain."

In our new concept, death became gain in Jesus Christ. Few days ago, I was going to a person for condolences after the death of a beloved one. When I told him that death transfers us to heaven, he said, "No, father, death is a gain." Actually, when he said these words, amidst his grief, I discovered rare faith. I said to myself that is the level a Christian should reach. Death is gain. We do not fear death, weariness, illness, position or even any person. We have Christ, our Life.

On the other hand, there is the narrow heart, full of grudges, jealousy and envy, like the hearts of the Pharisees, Scribes and Herod. The hearts of the world is full of disputes, battles and sufferings. If you enter any of these narrow hearts, you will find them poor in love. One of the fathers said: "In the manger, our Lord Jesus Christ had a covenant of love with humanity forever." The unlimited capabilities of God's love are added to our weak capabilities of love, so I, the destitute person, whose heart is full of weaknesses, envy, evil and narrowness, will discover unlimited richness and wideness in Christ Jesus.

In the past, I loved only my family, relatives and friends. Yet after the Lord's grace entered my heart, I now love those who hurt me and I love to the second mile. I feel satisfied in Jesus Christ who has given me a wide heart. I say with St Stephen, "Lord, do not charge them with this sin."

The Feast of Epiphany

The Feast of Epiphany—celebrating the public manifestation at His baptism of the Incarnate Son of God—follows closely our celebration of the Nativity of our Lord Jesus Christ. In the Nativity we have joy in the fact that our Lord is born as a human like us, taking our body and nature. As we have mentioned previously, when Christ took on our nature He blessed it through the unity of His divine nature. He shared everything with humanity, except our sin. While the Scriptures do not say much about the life of Jesus before His public ministry, it is clear that He lived as a perfect person.

Church history indicates that Saint Joseph the carpenter may have died when Jesus was 15 years old. Jesus then is likely to have taken over responsibility for the family business, working as a carpenter and sharing with us the weariness and toil of life.

Revealed to the world

At the age of 30, Jesus began His public ministry in obedience to His heavenly Father. His divine nature began to be revealed to everyone around him. He started this period by being baptised at the hands of John the Baptist. John was baptising many people and they received the forgiveness of sins after they had confessed. The Spirit revealed to John that Jesus was coming to be baptised by his hands, and at first, he refused. However Jesus said to him, "Permit it to be so now, for thus it is fitting for us to fulfil all righteousness." (Matthew 3:15)

While others came to John to be baptised, forgiven and cleansed, what could possibly Jesus be cleansed of? This is where we hear this heartfelt expression from John: "Behold! The Lamb of God who takes away the sin of the world!" (John 1:21) Jesus did not commit any sin, but He carried sin on behalf of all mankind. Baptism reveals to us that the carrying of our sins did not only occur on the cross, but was something He had done since His birth. He is the Lamb of God taking away the sin of the world. He is described as a Lamb because He is meek and came specifically for this mission to give His life. Jesus said, "I have trodden the wine press alone." (Isaiah 63:3) He is the only one who was "pressed" and knows the full bitterness of sin.

The Lord Creator asks John the Baptist, a created person,

to baptise Him. John says, "But you are not a sinner." Jesus answers, "Count me among the sinners." Imagine Jesus, standing in the row with the sinners, waiting for His turn to be baptised. We might ask, "Why would you do that my Lord? What compelled You?" He answers, "My love for you compelled me. I choose to die on your behalf and carry all your troubles."

Love beyond comprehension

No matter how much we meditate on the love of Jesus towards us, we can never fully comprehend the extent of that love. We know Adam and Eve sinned, were naked and ashamed, and without grace. God has responded by becoming naked so as to clothe the children of Adam and Eve with His grace. At the cross, the Lord was stripped naked, His hands were nailed instead of our filthy, sinful hands; He was spat on, blasphemed, insulted and cursed.

In this we see the Lamb of God bearing the sins of the world. In the Feast of Epiphany, we come to find the Lamb of God bearing the sins of the entire world. Christ is on the altar and we come to throw upon Him all our troubles, sins, ailments, and sufferings. If we are to hold on to these things our presence at the Liturgy is useless.

Children of God

Another blessing given to us in the mystery of baptism

is that we are born from God. While Jesus was being baptised in the Jordan River heaven was opened. The Holy Spirit descended upon our human nature in the person of Jesus Christ, and in this way the Holy Spirit descended on us all. When heaven was opened, a voice came down saying: "This is my beloved Son." (Matthew 3:17) As long as Jesus is God's 'beloved Son' and He shares the same human nature and body as we do, then we are His brothers and sisters in receiving this blessing.

In the fullness of time, God sent His Son, born of a woman who was under the Law, to redeem those who were under the Law. As mentioned, we are all brothers and sisters with Him through the same flesh, and also received adoption as children of God.

The Bible repeatedly assures us of this fact, the whole of Christianity rests on this profound truth. We are children born from our Lord. Whoever reads the Epistles of Saint John the Beloved will notice that he frequently repeats this phrase, "Born from God":

Whoever has been born of God does not sin, for His seed remains in him; and he cannot sin, because he has been born of God. Whoever does not practice righteousness is not of God, nor is he who does not love his brother. For this is the message that you heard from the beginning, that we should love one another. Do not marvel, my brethren, if the world hates you. We know that we have passed from death to life, because we love the brethren. He who does not love his brother abides in death. Whoever hates his brother is a murderer, and you know that no murderer has eternal life abiding in him. 1 John 3:9-11, 13-14

During the Feast of Epiphany, as we celebrate the baptism of Jesus, we should remember our own baptism because He was baptised for our sake. Nicodemus came to Him at night to inquire about receiving eternal life, saying to Jesus, "you are a teacher who has come from God. For no one could perform the signs you are doing if God were not with him." Jesus answered him, "Most assuredly I say to you, unless one is born again, he cannot see the kingdom of God." (John 3:2-3) Here the Bible portrays the single most important message of the Church; that we should repent and be baptised.

One baptism, ongoing repentance

In the early days when the practice was to baptise adults, it was preceded by the condition of repentance and faith. When we baptise a baby, the condition is that his father and mother should be repentant. The parents should bring the child up in the fear of God. We have confidence that He who is born from God can overcome the world. Saint John says, "But as many as received Him, to them He gave power to become children of God, to those who believe in His name: who were born, not of blood, nor of the will of the flesh, nor of the will of man, but of God." (John 1:12, 13)

We read in the Bible that because we are born from God and are children of God, the world hates us even as it first hated our Lord. If this sonship is not clear in our life, we should offer repentance. Baptism cannot be repeated, it occurs only once, but repentance is an ongoing process. The church fathers considered repentance as a type of second baptism, as seen in the example of the Prodigal Son who finally repented and returned to his father. . If we want to enjoy the blessings of repentance gained through our childhood baptism, we are to offer true, ongoing repentance to our Lord.

The sons and daughters of God will have the same characteristics as their Father. It is good to ask ourselves if our lives demonstrate the characteristics of Jesus'. Our hope is that just as when we came away from the baptismal font wearing white clothes, that likewise in Christ in eternity we will wear the same white clothes.

While being sojourners on earth, between baptism and eternity, our call is to retain the purity of our 'clothes'. In doing this though, it is important to keep the right perspective. It is incorrect to think our life on earth is the main event! On the contrary, life in heaven is the real priority. When we lose sight of this perspective, our sonship with the Lord Jesus loses direction and strength,

A challenge to proper living

We should remember that the early church lived with a very real sense that God is near and that Jesus was coming again soon. We too can live with this same earnest expectation.

We know Jesus is always opening His heart to receive sinners. The image of Him hanging on the cross is always before our eyes. We see His arms stretched wide as He says, "Come to Me all you who labour and are heavy laden, and I will give you rest." (Matthew 11:28) In order to enter the blessings of this feast, we are called to approach Jesus with repentance, to return to our first love.

The challenge to live a life of repentance seems to grow harder in our modern day society. We might ask, where is the love mentioned in the Bible? "And because lawlessness will abound, the love of many will grow cold." (Matthew 24:12). And elsewhere, "Whoever hates his brother is a murderer, he who is born of God loves his brother, and he who hates his brother is not born of God." (1 John 3)

The challenges for our young people are even greater. The beautiful modesty and gentleness of the Christian youth are constantly under pressure. The Feast of Epiphany is a time to return to life demonstrating the characteristics of the Virgin and the Christ. It is always good to ask ourselves and each other, are we conquering the world or is it conquering us? Are we yielding ourselves bit by bit to the world?

In a book written about 20 years ago by the late Bishop Athanasius of Beni Sweif, he speaks to his congregation about modesty and coming to Church. In particular he speaks to the girls in gentle words about how they are made in the image of Christ, and that clothes are created to cover us, rather than the contrary. If he felt it necessary to speak these words 20 years ago, what might his reaction be today?

As for parents, grandparents and older members of the church, one should ask, "what are we doing to encourage the youth of the church to share in the characteristics of our Lord Jesus, and to help them overcome the authority of the world"?

A spiritual celebration

The Feast of Epiphany, though often celebrated as a religious formality, should indeed be celebrated in spirit. We cannot deceive God with many fasts, sacrifices or offerings. God is looking for purity of the heart, as mentioned by David the Prophet; "Godly sorrow brings repentance that leads to salvation and leaves no regret, but worldly sorrow brings death." (2 Corinthians 7:10) This is our Christianity; this is how we observe the Feast of Epiphany. We are reborn as the children of God, baptised into His body, and are called to keep our baptism clothes clean.

Beyond this, we are also called to be witnesses for Christ in the world. We should hope that people identify that we are the children of Christ as soon as they meet us. This is despite being aware that temptation is around us everywhere, fiercer than in any other age—on television, on our phones and internet, in fashion and popular culture and even in our homes. However, we can be assured that sincere witnessing the glory of God, with people offering their lives on the altar of sacrifice because of their love of Christ the King, will not cease. This is why we need a repentant church, always coming back to the Lord seeking purity of heart, and yearning to see God.

Final words

As we conclude this chapter and our entire book that has examined the Incarnation and reflected on the Feast of Annunciation, Nativity and Epiphany, let us be reminded of a gift which we can offer the Lord.

These Feasts provide ideal opportunities in which to open our hearts to Christ and pray to him:

"O my Lord, You were born in the manger, come now

and be born inside our heart. If our heart is defiled, You are the One who is able to purify it through Your power and grace. If the world and its temptation are strong on us, You give us the power of victory through Jesus Christ. If evil is surrounding us, 'He who is with us is stronger than those against us.' We believe that You are dwelling in the midst of us. We believe Lord that You are the source of love, purity, peace and joy in the church. Our Gracious Father, please hear our prayers and repentance, granting us freedom and joy to celebrate our spiritual feasts."

www.ingramcontent.com/pod-product-compliance
Lightning Source LLC
Chambersburg PA
CBHW021912040426
42447CB00007B/816

9 780099 457108 3